101 Amazir
Do in C

© 2018 101 Amazing Things

All rights reserved. No part of this publication may be reproduced, distributed, or transmitted in any form or by any means, including photocopying, recording, or other electronic or mechanical methods, without the prior written permission of the publisher, except in the case of brief quotations embodied in critical reviews and certain other noncommercial uses permitted by copyright law.

Introduction

So you're going to Colombia, huh? You are very very lucky indeed! You are sure in for a treat because Colombia is truly one of the most magical countries on the face of the earth.

We will take you on a journey through all of the most popular places in the country, such as Bogota, Medellin, Cartagena, Cali, Popayan islands such as the San Bernardo Islands, and even deep into the Colombian Amazon jungle.

In this guide, we'll be giving you the low down on:
- the very best things to shove in your pie hole, from street food staples like gorgeous arepas stuffed with cheese through to gourmet ceviche in Cartagena
- the best shopping so that you can take a little piece of Colombia back home with you, whether that's in the form of some strong Colombian coffee or original artwork from a local gallery
- incredible festivals, whether you'd prefer to celebrate all the colour of Carnival in Barranquilla, or you fancy attending a massive rock festival in Bogota

- the coolest historical and cultural sights that you simply cannot afford to miss from ancient funerary complexes through to contemporary art galleries
- outstanding experiences in nature from white water rafting on the River Suarez through to visiting a flamingo sanctuary
- and tonnes more coolness besides!

Let's not waste any more time – here are the 101 most amazing, spectacular, and cool things not to miss in Colombia!

Long Trek to the Lost City

rue adventurer, the one thing you absolutely hile in Colombia is trek to the Lost City. This is a trek of four to six days, and it will take you through the incredibly scenic Sierra Nevada Mountains, which leads to the Lost City, a place that has been dubbed the New Machu Piccu. You will get to trek about 46 kilometres of varied landscapes, from jungle to mountain peaks and river valleys too. The trek is not always easy, but it's so incredibly rewarding – not just when you reach the end, but every moment along the way.

2. Eat a Traditional Cali Dish: Arroz Atollado

As you travel around Colombia, you are likely to notice that the food will change from place to place, and we think that the city of Cali in the southwest of the country is a place with a truly incredible gastronomic scene. One dish that you won't want to miss while you're in Cali is Arroz Atollado, which you can think of as a hearty mixed rice dish. You'll get a bowlful of rice mixed with chicken pork, vegetables, and seasonings like coriander, cumin, garlic, and cloves.

3. Improve Your Spanish Skills

If you only have a few words of Spanish, you will probably be able to get by on your trip to Colombia, but you will feel frustrated. If you have a longer period of time in the country, take at least a week and have some intensive Spanish classes so that you can actually communicate, and get to know the local people so much better. Colombia is actually one of the best places to learn Spanish because Colombians tends to speak correctly and clearly. One of our favourite Spanish schools in the country is Amazon Spanish College because of its location in the jungle. *(www.amazonspanishcollege.com)*

4. Enjoy a Weekend Getaway on Isla Grande

Cartagena is a lovely coastal place in Colombia, but it draws a lot of crowds, and if you fancy something of a weekend escape, Isla Grande is the place to go to. Not so many tourists come here so you will get to have a more tranquil experience, and perhaps have one of the beautiful beaches of the island all to yourself. There is also a bird sanctuary on the island if you happen to be a birdwatcher.

5. Shop for Treasures at a Bogota Flea Market

If you want to have a really authentic shopping experience while you're in Colombia, ditch the tourist joints and head to the local markets instead. A Bogota flea market you really have to check out is called Mercado de las Pulgas de San Alejo, and opens to the public every Sunday to showcase a whole range of goodies. Over 300 vendors show up each week, and sell things as far reaching as vintage posters, jewellery, and bizarre items that could make fantastic souvenirs.

(Cra. 7 #24-70, Bogotá; www.pulgassanalejo.co)

6. Hike Through the Valle de Cocora

Colombia is a country with plenty of greenery, which makes it a spectacular destination for people who love to strap on their hiking boots and spend plenty of time in the great outdoors. And one of the most perfectly green and lush places is the Valle de Cocora. The good news is that you don't have to be an athlete for this hike, and it will take you 6 hours maximum to complete. The highlight of the trek is getting to see the gigantic wax palms of Colombia, which are the tallest palms in the world.

7. Help Out a Sweet Tooth With Bunelos

It seems that every place in the world we visit has its own version of the humble (but very delicious) doughnut, and Colombia is no exception. If you have any leanings toward the sweet side of life, you are going to love Colombian bunelos. What's really interesting about these rounds of fried batter is that they have a salty sweet mix. As well as sugar, you will find a kind of grated salty white cheese inside. These are typically served around Christmas, but you can find them at any time of year.

8. Immerse Yourself in Coffee Culture on a Coffee Farm

Coffee lovers are in for a huge treat while in Colombia, but if you really want to get under the skin of the country's coffee culture, don't just drink the stuff but make your way to the coffee farms to see how it's produced and how it creates a way of life for so many Colombians in the hills. One place we heartily recommend visiting is called Hacienda Venecia. This hacienda has won numerous awards for its coffee, and they also offer walks through the plantation and classes in coffee preparation. You can also stay there if you really want to immerse yourself in coffee. *(Manizales, Caldas; www.haciendavenecia.com)*

9. Take in the Bizarre Yipao Jeep Parade

When we visit a new country, we love to explore the slightly stranger parts of the local culture, and boy is the Yipao Jeep Parade something strange. In the coffee growing hills of Colombia you see jeeps everywhere. A benefit of the jeep is that it can be loaded up with so much stuff, and that's what this parade is all about. The jeeps are loaded up with as much as humanly possible, and then paraded through the streets of Quindio to the delight of the local population.

10. Get Opulent at Bogota's Gold Museum

If you're feeling especially opulent, the Gold Museum is the place to visit in Bogota. Although this is a very niche museum, it's one of the most visited and most popular museums in all of Colombia, with half a million visitors every year. The Gold Museum is seriously blingtastic, with more than 55,000 pieces of gold inside. There are pieces from around Colombia and Latin America, with objects such as gold offerings, animal figurines, and jewellery. *(Cra. 6 #15-88, Bogotá; www.banrepcultural.org/bogota/museo-del-oro)*

11. Have a Paragliding Adventure Over the Chicamocha Canyon

La Chichamocha in Colombia is a place of extraordinary beauty, and is otherwise known as The Grand Canyon of Colombia. The landscape is nothing short of breath taking, and if you are an adventure seeker, you can enjoy this unique landscape in a way that is particularly adrenaline pumping. Between 9am and noon every morning, you can paraglide over this incredible natural wonder. Because of the depth of the canyon, your flight is double the height of most paragliding adventures – an experience that is truly once in a lifetime.

12. Watch a Football Match at Estadio El Campin

Colombians are absolutely crazy about football (soccer). You will see youngsters kicking balls around in the parks, and you'll hear roars coming from bars as people watch matches live. But none of that compares to actually seeing a football match in one of the stadiums across the country. While you're in Bogota, be sure to buy tickets for a game at the Estadio El Campin, the largest stadium in the city. When the whole of the 67,000 seater stadium is full, the atmosphere is electric.

(Carrera 30 y Calle 57, Bogotá, Cundinamarca; www.idrd.gov.co/sitio/idrd/?q=node/516)

13. Eat Colombian Ceviche in Cartagena

When you think of mouth watering ceviche, you would probably think of Peru, but Colombia also has its own ceviche, and it is particularly prevalent along the coast. The place to really chow down in Cartagena is a restaurant called La Cevicheria, made famous because Anthony Bourdain once ate there – and because the food is just really good. As well as ceviche, they also serve up a fruity tropical paella, and delicious sangria.

(Cl. 39 #7 14, Cartagena, http://lacevicheriacartagena.com)

14. Join a Free Graffiti Tour in Bogota

Bogota is an exciting city that changes all the time, and one place where you can really see that change is in the art that you can find on the city streets. Something fantastic about Colombia is that it doesn't treat street artists as delinquents and criminals but as true talent that deserves to be recognised. You can, of course, walk the streets and see this art at any time, but we recommend joining the Bogota Graffiti Tour, which will really give you the inside track on this movement. It's free so you really have nothing to lose.

(http://bogotagraffiti.com)

15. Rent a Hammock for the Night in Tayrona National Park

Colombia has something for every kind of traveller, and if you love nothing more than to connect with all the beauty of nature, you are in luck. One of the most gorgeous spots in the country is Tayrona National Park. This is a very special place because it combines thick rainforest with mangroves and sandy beaches. Arrecifes beach is a highlight of the park where you can rent a hammock for the night. You might have an achy back in the morning, but you will have never felt more connected to nature.

(www.parquesnacionales.gov.co/portal/es/ecoturismo/region-caribe/parque-nacional-natural-tayrona)

16. Go Scuba Diving off Isla de Providencia

For a taste of the Colombian Caribbean, it really gets no better than a small island called Isla de Providencia. This island is part of Colombia but it's actually close to Nicaragua, and a wonderful place to truly get away from it all. Providencia is very unspoiled and it's a superb place to relax on the beaches (with virtually nobody around), but because this place is so isolated, the waters are incredible, and the diving is really second to none. There are plenty of diving companies here that will take you out in the water, even if you have no prior experience.

17. Have an Artsy Day at the Museum of Antioquia

Arts lovers need to know about the Museum of Antioquia, which is one of the most celebrated art museums in all of Colombia. This gallery is located on the campus of the University of Antioquia, and has more than 60,000 art pieces on display. There really is something for everyone here, because you will find pre-Columbian, colonial, and modern artwork. Keep your eyes peeled on their programme of events too, because you might catch a cool dance show or exhibition opening.

(Cl. 52 #52-43, Medellín, Antioquia; www.museodeantioquia.co)

18. Get Back to Nature at Los Flamencos Sanctuary

Located on the Caribbean coast of Colombia, Los Flamencos Sanctuary is a must visit for all animal and nature lovers. This is a huge nature reserve that comprises marshes, lagoons, and dry forests, and the diversity of the landscapes means that it attracts an equally diverse amount of birdlife. As you might expect from the name of the place, the stars of the show are the flamingos – and you will see them in the hundreds. But you will also find hummingbirds, puff birds, cardinals, and many other bird species besides.

19. Tuck Into Arepas From the Streets

Colombia is a country with a huge array of delicious food, and the great news is that you don't have to spend a fortune in fancy restaurants to eat like a King. Street food abounds in Colombia, and one of the most popular things to eat on the street is an arepa. These are essentially a type of thick yellow corn cake, that can either be topped or stuffed with things like cheese, eggs, meat, and cream.

20. Explore a 17th Century Fortress in Cartagena

You might think of Colombia as more of a destination for great parties and experiences in nature, but history buffs aren't left out on a trip to Colombia either. If you have a passion for history, one sight you cannot miss is Castillo San Felipe de Barajas in Cartagena, a fortress that dates way back to the 16th century. This is the greatest fortress built by the Spanish in any one of their colonies, and it still dominates on the skyline of the city. Be sure to take the audio tour through the spooky tunnels of the fortress.
(Cra. 17, Cartagena; http://fortificacionescartagena.com/en)

21. Go Back to the Cretaceous Period at the Museo El Fosil

There are some great museums dotted around Colombia, and one of the strangest of the lot is the Fossil museum. Villa de Leyva is a colonial town in the hills of Colombia, and all around the town there are fossils that point back to prehistoric times. The museum here showcases the wares of what has been found from around the town, and the most impressive specimen is a 7 metre long, 15 million year old Kronosaurus - a distant relative of the modern crocodile.

(www.museoelfosil.org)

22. Visit a Cathedral Carved Out of Salt

Since Colombia is a Catholic country, you will get to see many churches as you travel around, but none are quite as unique as the Catedral de Dal de Zipaquira, which is an underground chapel totally constructed within an underground salt mine. If you want to enter this cathedral, you will have to venture 200 metres underground, where you can take your time walking through the 14 fluorescently lit chapels.

(Parque De La Sal, Zipaquirá; www.catedraldesal.gov.co)

23. Take a Pablo Escobar Tour in Medellin

Pablo Escobar is a name that you are probably familiar with. He was the head honcho when it came to drug cartels in Colombia. Fortunately, the government has done an incredible job dealing with the narco groups, but Pablo Escobar is still a name with a lot of resonance in Colombia. And in Medellin, you can even go on a Pablo Escobar Tour around the city. You'll learn about the life and death of Escobar, who was once the 7th richest man in the world.

(http://pabloescobartour.co)

24. Stroll the Aisles of the Central Cemetery of Bogota

Okay, we know that walking around a graveyard probably isn't going to be at the very top of your to-do list while you're in Colombia, but we do think that the Central Cemetery of Bogota is something special and worth checking out if you have the time. This is the most famous cemetery in all of Colombia, and many important people have been laid to rest there. Among the tombstones, you will find former presidents like Santos Acosta, and poets like Rafael Pombo.

(Cra. 20 #3780, Bogotá)

25. Be Wowed by La Chorrera Waterfall

While Colombia is not a country that is famed for its stunning waterfalls, there are some waterfalls to be found, and we think that La Chorrera might be the most impressive of the lot. Many people don't realise that there is gorgeous countryside around Bogota, and this is where you'll find La Chorrera. This is Colombia's highest waterfall with a drop of 590 metres, and watching the water gush down from the base of the falls is nothing short of breath taking.

26. Party With Locals at Medellin's My Sweet Jesus

Colombians love to party, so if you fancy dancing the night away, you'll pretty much have the opportunity to do so on any night of the week. One of the most popular clubs in Medellin is called Dulce Jesus Mio, or My Sweet Jesus. We can't pretend that this is the coolest place on the block, but it's absolutely the most fun. It has a kitsch feel, the music is fun, and everyone there will drag you on to the dancefloor and make sure that you have the time of your life.

(Carrera 38 #19 255, Medellín; http://fondadulcejesusmio.com)

27. Be Stunned by Cano Cristales, the River of Five Colours

There are certain parts of Colombia that nature lovers simply can't afford to miss, and Cano Cristales might just be at the very top of that list. This river is located in the Macarena province, and also goes by the name of The River of Five Colours. Pay a visit and you will soon understand why that is. During a certain time of year, the river positively explodes with colour. A bright red flower lines the riverbed, turning the water red, and you will also find splotches of green plant life, yellow sand, and blue water.

28. Tuck Into the Delicious Breakfast Soup of Changua

As the saying goes, breakfast is the most important time of the day, so forget soggy cereal and boring toast, and enjoy a yummy bowl of changua for breakfast while you're in Colombia. This is most commonly found in the Central Andes region of the country, and it is a seasoned milk soup with a poached egg inside. The soup is simply topped with spring onions and coriander, and all mopped up with a piece of bread – a great way to start the day.

29. Go Souvenir Shopping at Pasaje Rivas Craft Market

There is no doubt that you'll want to take back lots of things from Colombia to remind you of your time in this incredible country, and a great place to do all your gift shopping in one spot is the Pasaje Rivas Craft Market in Bogota. This market has been open for over a century, is absolutely jam packed with character, and not many tourists know about it. It's full of genuine Colombian made things like Colombian ponchos, handmade ceramics, and loads more besides.

(Carrera 10 No. 10 - 54, Bogotá)

30. Have a Fun Filled Day at Hacienda Napoles

Travelling with kids is a double edged sword. On the one hand, it's a privilege to be able to show them foreign countries and provide them with wonderful memories, but keeping kids entertained around the clock is also a very difficult task. One place they are sure to have tonnes of fun is a waterpark called Hacienda Napoles. Inside you will also find models of giant dinosaurs, and real exotic animals like tigers and alligators. And just an FYI, this place was originally created by Pablo Escobar.

(Kilómetro 165 de la, Autopista Medellín-Bogotá, Puerto Triunfo, Doradal; www.haciendanapoles.com)

31. Indulge a Bibliophile at the Bogota International Book Fair

Are you something of a bibliophile? Then the Bogota International Book Fair is sure to be right up your alley. This event is no little book fair – it is absolutely gargantuan. You can expect over 1200 events that represent over 20 countries around the world, and around half a million people attend! You'll have the chance to meet with authors, get your books signed, attend workshops with writers and publishers, and, of course, purchase lots and lots of books. The fair has been running for over 30 years, and takes place each year in April or May.

(https://feriadellibro.com)

32. Take a Mud Bath at Volcan de Lodo el Totumo

Ever wanted to jump into the bubbling crater of a volcano? Probably not. But we guarantee that Volcan de Lodo el Totumo will be the exception. This mini volcano is located around 50 kilometres from Cartagena, but instead of bubbling molten lava, you can find bubbling mud spewing from this volcano. You can actually climb into the volcano and take a mud bath, which is said to do wonders for your skin, and then wash the mud off in the lagoon next door.

33. Ascend El Penon de Guatape

Guatape is a lovely little town located around two hours from Medellin, and it is famous for one thing. Drive into the town and you won't fail to notice it – a giant rock called El Penon de Guatape. This huge stone was formed millions of years ago and was worshipped by the Tahamies Indians who lived there. There's a steep set of steps that can take you all the way to the top – 659 steps in total. We can't say that this climb is an easy one, but the view from the top is really quite something.

34. Get to Grips With the History of Sugarcane in Palmira

One of the most interesting museums that you can visit during your time in Colombia is the Sugarcane Museum in Palmira, outside of Cali. You can see sugarcane fields throughout the landscapes of Valle del Cauca, and here is where you will learn more about the importance and the history of sugar on this region. The museum is an old hacienda filled with machinery and lot of information pertaining to the production of sugar.

(Corregimiento Santa Elena, vereda Amaimito a 8 Kms de el crucero de El, Placer, Valle del Cauca; www.museocanadeazucar.com)

35. Hike the Camino Real From Barichara to Guane

If you love to be outdoors but you don't want to take part in any adventurous activities that are too taxing on the body, a 10 kilometre hike along the Camino Real between the town of Barichara and Guane is a really great option. The hike is mostly downhill, but not dramatically so, so it should be okay as long as your knees are in decent condition. You'll experience lush green, total peace and quiet apart from birdsong and the occasional local child playing, and a goat or five.

36. Indulge a History Buff at Cartagena's Palace of the Inquisition

In many ways, Cartagena is the historic and cultural capital of Colombia, and history enthusiasts won't want to miss a trip to the Palace of the Inquisition. This was built in 1770 as the Holy Seat of the Inquisition, and now serves as a museum space. This is one of the finest examples of colonial architecture in Cartagena with a grand Baroque entrance, and a very beautiful courtyard filled with lush green and detailed tile work. The museum collection is somewhat more grisly, specialising in instruments of torture.

(46 Plaza de Bolivar, Cra. 3 #33, Cartagena)

37. Rock Out at Rock al Parque

If you love nothing more to dance in the open air to live music, you might be tempted by festivals like Benicassim or Primavera Sound, but Colombia also has a thriving, if somewhat unknown, festival scene. Rock al Parque takes place in Bogota each year in July, and it's considered the biggest rock festival in all of Colombia, attracting over 400,000 attendees. The focus is on Latin American rock, but bands such as Bloc Party and Black Rebel Motorcycle Club have also performed.

(www.rockalparque.gov.co)

38. Look at the Shakira Monument That Looks Nothing Like Shakira

Colombia has had a huge influence upon the world culturally with many poets, writers, and musicians coming from the country. Bringing things up to date, perhaps the most famous singer from Colombia internationally is…. Shakira. Her hips don't liee but the statue built in her honour in her hometown of Barranquilla kinda does. It was a nice thought, but this metal statue truly looks nothing like the Latina singer.

39. Enjoy a Game of Tejo in Salento

Ever heard of a game called tejo before? Don't worry because you are not the only one, but tejo is a traditional sport in Colombia, the origins of which are not really

known. The basic idea is to hurl a metal disc into a box 20 metres away. The exciting twist is that there are explosives inside the box that get set off when a person scores. If you fancy playing the game yourself, there is a centre called Los amigos in Salento where you can do exactly that.
(Cra. 6 #6 21, Salento)

40. Feed Monkeys at Micos Monkey Island

The small town of Leticia is your gateway to the thick jungle of the Amazon, and while there don't miss out on a trip to Isla de los Micos, or Monkey Island – a place that is home to more than 5000 playful primates. You'll go with a guide so don't worry about being mauled by monkeys, but you should know that if you don't like close contact with animals this might not be the place for you, because you will have monkeys literally all over you at any given time. For animal lovers, it's a very special trip.

41. Enjoy a Big Plate of Lechona

If you love nothing more than to tuck into a delicious meat roast, we have a feeling that you will appreciate the yumminess of Colombian lechona very much indeed. This is essentially a hog roast, but it's a little more involved than a hog roast you'd have back home. The meat is forked off the animal and mixed with garlic and spring onions, which is then mixed with yellow peas and rice and put back into the animal to roast. Simply delicious.

42. Descend Into San Gil's Cow Cave

La Cueva de la Vaca, or Cow's Cave, is a place that adventurers in Colombia are sure to love. The cave is located in San Gil, in the northeast of the country, and it features a series of narrow passageways and tight spots that add up to a really incredible caving experience – but one that would be unsuitable for the faint of heart. There are portions where you will need to slide across the cave floor, and parts that require diving underwater. In the final cave, you'll be rewarded by finding yourself in a cave full of stalactites hanging from the roof.

43. Cool Down With a Cholado Colombiano

Colombia is a huge country – much more expansive than it looks from glancing at a map – and some parts of the country can be very warm indeed. When you need to cool down, the most fun way to do so is with a Cholado Colombiano, which is an icy beverage native to Colombia. Inside, you will typically find shaved ice, chopped fruits, condensed milk, fruit syrup, and sometimes whipped cream. The fruits most typically used are banana, kiwi, strawberry, coconut, papaya, and pineapple.

44. Enjoy a Gondola Ride in Arvi Park

Medellin is a really incredible city, but when you feel as though you need to escape city life for a moment, the place to go to is Arvi Park. There are quite a few walking trails in the park, but our favourite thing to do is take a gondola ride. Arvi Park is the beginning of the gondola ride, and from there it will take you over the park and across the city. It's cheap and the view is second to none.

45. Crumble Cheese on Your Hot Chocolate in Bogota

When you think of Colombia, you might think of a very warm country, and it definitely can be warm, but in Bogota, the capital city, it can get really quite chilly. We don't know about you, but when we need to warm up, we immediately crave hot chocolate. Fortunately, hot chocolate is very easy to find in Bogota, but the locals have rather an odd way of consuming their hot chocolate – by crumbling cheese on top. The cheese gets all melty and mingles with the chocolate to create and sweet and savoury treat that is much better than it sounds.

46. Go Snorkelling at El Cabo San Juan Beach

Colombia has so much going on that it's not primarily thought of as a beach destination, but there are some truly stunning beaches dotted around the country. Lazy beach days can be great, but if you fancy more active beach days, you can spend time in the beautifully clear waters by snorkelling. Our favourite beach for this is El Cabo San Juan, which you will find within Tayrona National Park. You will find yourself surrounded by beautiful tropical fish in clear water.

47. Check out the Sculptures in Botero Plaza

One of the lovely things about Medellin is that it's a city that has all the benefits of city living, but also with plenty of green and open space. One of our favourite plazas is called Botero Plaza, where you can find plenty of people hanging out in the daytime. The really charming thing about this plaza is that it contains 23 abstract sculptures by Colombian artist Fernando Botero, acting just like an open air museum in the middle of the city.

(Carabobo, Medellín)

48. Learn Something New at the Colombian National Museum

There is tonnes of exciting stuff to see and do in Colombia, but while you are outside looking at ruins and churches, it can be great to have some background knowledge about what you are seeing. For the best history lesson, a morning spent at the Colombian National Museum in Bogota is a very good idea. The museum is particularly strong on prehistoric artefacts, and you will find some things that date back as far as 10,000 BC. You can learn about Colombian ceramics, painting, and much more besides.

(N, Cra. 7a #28-66, Bogotá; www.museonacional.gov.co)

49. Pass an Afternoon at the Medellin Museum of Modern Art

For artsy visitors in Colombia, the Medellin Museum of Modern Art is an absolute must-visit gallery. As you would expect, the focus here is on contemporary art pieces, so don't expect to see anything from the Masters of Colombia. There is also a great focus placed on local work, so it's a good place to get to grips with the Colombian art scene. Do check out their programme of events for screenings and performances too.

(Carrera 44 #19A-100, Avenida de las Vegas Ciudad del Río, Medellín; www.elmamm.org)

50. Enjoy the Rich Sweetness of Natilla Pudding

If you have any kind of sweet tooth, you must try natilla while you are in Colombia. This sweet and creamy pudding is traditionally served at Christmas time, but you can seek it out at any time of the year. If you are a fan of creamy desserts like crème brulee, you will really adore this. It is essentially a sweet custard, but it is flavoured with coconut and cinnamon to make it extra delicious.

51. Explore the Subterranean Tombs of Tierradentro

If you have any interest in history or adventure (or both!), Tierradentro, an archaeological park in the Cauca department of Colombia, is an absolute must visit. This park consists of a series of subterranean tombs that were created around the year 700AD but were only discovered and excavated in the mid 20th century. This funeral complex dates back thousands of years, but you can still see the brightly coloured painted walls inside.

52. Purchase Fairtrade Handicrafts from Mambe

Before you depart from Colombia, you will surely want to purchase some things that will remind you of this extraordinary country, and you might need to do some gift shopping too. Avoid the tourist traps, and head to a charming shop called Mambe in Bogota instead. This shop specialises in the handicrafts of Colombia, and everything inside is made by the hands of people in rural communities around the country. You'll be able to pick up things like ceramics, hand woven baskets, and exquisite jewellery.
(23, Cra. 5 #117, Bogotá;
www.mambe.org/index.php/en/mambe-shop-en)

53. Indulge a Caffeine Addiction at the Panorama Café Hostel

Colombia is a coffee lover's wet dream. As well as sipping on plenty of delicious Colombian coffee, you can ramp up the coffee loving experience by spending a night or two at the Panorama Café Hostel in Quindio. The hostel has incredible views of the coffee plantations in the lush green hills of the region, and as you might expect, there is always incredible piping hot Colombian coffee on tap.

(Cra. 7 #328, Buenavista, Quindío; www.experienciacafetera.com/es/sugerencia/panorama-cafe-hostel)

54. Get to Grips With Colombian Art at Miguel Urrutia Art Museum

Because Medellin in seen as the hipster alternative to Bogota, you might think that it's the city for an artsy time, but Bogota has its fair share or arts culture too, and a gallery not to miss is the Miguel Urrutia Art Museum. This is the place to get to grips with Colombian art, and there is a lot of space dedicated to the celebrated local artist,

Fernando Botero. If you enjoyed his sculptures in Botero Plaza, this is the museum for you.
(Calle 11 #4-21, La Candelaria, Bogotá; www.banrepcultural.org/bogota/museo-botero)

55. Enjoy the Stunning Beaches of Isla Mucura

If you are the kind of person who loves the simplicity of stretching out on the sand and hearing the waves lap up against the shore, be sure to visit some of Colombia's islands. Isla Mucura is just a two hour boat ride away from Cartagena, but in spite of this it is not really known as a major destination in Colombia. This means that it's a true escape. You won't find lots of restaurants or nightlife, and for us it's the beauty of the place.

56. Stroll Through the Botanical Garden of Medellin

Medellin is a very liveable pleasant city – not too big and not too small – but when you really feel like you just want perfect greenery and pure silence, the Joaquin Antonio Uribe botanical gardens are the place to be. With more than 4500 flowers, this is a paradise for nature lovers. Enter the gardens and you will find a butterfly house where the butterflies flutter all around you, a cactus garden, a pond area, and even a library.

(Cl. 73 #51d14, Medellín; www.botanicomedellin.org)

57. Learn How to Salsa Like a Latino

If you head out to any bar or club in Colombia, you are sure to notice that the local people sure do know how to move their bodies, and if you would like to salsa just like a Latino, it can be well worth investing in salsa classes while you are in the country. DANCEFREE is a dance school in Medellin that is foreigner friendly and beginner friendly too. So now you have no excuses not to take to the dancefloor.

(Calle 10A #40-27, El Poblado, Medellín; www.dancefree.com.co)

58. Indulge a Science Geek at the Maloka Museum

Colombia has a diverse selection of art museums, but what if you're more of a science geek than an art enthusiast? No worries because the Maloka Museum in Bogota was designed just for folks like you. The really great thing about this museum is that it's not just a place to see things inside of glass cabinets, but a place where almost every

part of the exhibitions is interactive. There are nine different rooms, each of which explores a different theme, such as the human body, the universe, and water.
(Cra. 68d #24A-51, Bogotá; www.maloka.org)

59. Sip on Cocktails at Huerta Bar Cocteleria Artesenal

Bogota is the definition of a happening city, and every cool city worth its weight needs to have a fine selection of bars. When you want to go somewhere where the drinks are that little bit more special than the average, we'd recommend Bar Cocteleria Artesenal, in our opinion the finest hotspot for a cocktail in Bogota. All ingredients used are 100% natural, much of which is made from scratch on-site. We love their take on a Negroni, which uses mezcal in place of gin, and a pineapple infused Campari.
(Cl. 69a #10-15, Bogotá; www.huertabar.com)

60. Enjoy the Semana Santa Celebrations of Popayan

Semana Santa, or the Holy Week, is a truly wonderful time to be in Colombia, with lots of celebrations throughout the country – but the ultimate Semana Santa destination has to be Popayan, located in the southwest of the country. It's here that you can find a number of daily religious processions that have taken place since the sixteenth century. Being in Popayan at this time is an incredible way to feel the weight and beauty of Colombian tradition.

61. Explore a World of Giant Oddities at Jaime Duque Park

When you feel overwhelmed with city life in Bogota, we recommend driving just half an hour outside of the city where you can find Jaime Duque Park. This park was opened in the 1980s with the intention of bringing the Wonders of the World to Colombia. And that is exactly what you will find. The highlight is a lifesize replica of the Taj Mahal – which is really strange to see in the middle of Colombia. You can also check out sights like Colossus of Rhodes and Russia's Red Square.

(Centro Comercial Hacienda Santa Bárbara, Cra. 7 #6A, Briceno, Bogotá; www.parquejaimeduque.com)

62. Slurp on a Big Bowl of Ajiaco in Bogota

Colombia is a pretty big country, and as you travel from place to place you are sure to notice that different food is eaten in different places. When in Bogota, we love to warm ourselves up with a heaped bowl of ajiaco. This is essentially a chicken and potato soup, made with three different kinds of potatoes that are found in Colombia, and a local herb. You might find some corn and avocado in there too. It's warm, hearty, and perfect for a chilly day in the Colombian capital.

63. Take a Day Trip to the San Bernardo Islands

So you're a beach lover, huh? Colombia might not strike you as the first place to travel to for lazy beach days, but the country actually has some very beautiful beaches, and did you know that there are also islands off the coast of the country that you can visit? If you just want to totally get away from the stresses of daily life for a day, we'd recommend a day-trip to the San Bernardo Islands, which can be reached from Cartagena by boat in just two hours. Our favourite of the ten islands is Tintipan, because of its incredible beaches and colourful buildings.

64. Wave a Rainbow Flag at Bogota's Gay Pride Event

Colombia is an interesting place politically because it can be thought of as both traditional and progressive at the same time. This is a Catholic country, but it's also a place where LGBT people are widely accepted, particularly in the large cities. You can get to grips with the colourful nature of the local gay scene in Bogota by attending their Gay Pride event, which takes place each year at the beginning of July. The peak of the celebration is a giant parade through the city.

65. Swim in the Waters of Marinka Waterfalls

Minca is a delightful little place in the Sierra Nevada of Colombia that has fresh temperatures, and lush green coffee farms – ideal for when you want to escape city life. And something else that you will find in this part of Colombia are the Marinka Waterfalls. This waterfall isn't a giant, with a drop of only about 20 metres, but what we love about it is the pool of freshwater that collects at the bottom – perfectly safe for swimming.

66. Eat a Gorgeous Platter of Bandeja Paisa

If you are a true foodie at heart, we heartily recommend tucking into a big plate of Bandeja Paisa, and what we love about this meal is that it involves so many different things on a plate that each bite is different, and you are sure to find something that you love on the platter. This meal typically consists of white rice, ground pork, red beans cooked with pork, black pudding, pork rinds, chorizo arepa, sauces, and avocado. Ordering this is a fantastic way of getting to grips with lots of the local delicacies, and you'll find it all over Colombia.

67. Learn About Urban Conflict of the City While in Medellin

Colombia is a beautiful country, but it is a place that has had a chequered past, and it can be well worth getting to grips with the violence that occurred in Medellin at the Museo Casa de la Memoria. Mainly because of the drug cartels, Medellin suffered bombings, kidnappings, bribes, threats, massacres, and more from the 1980s to the mid 1990s. This museum pays respect to the victims during that period, and tells their stories.

(Cl. 51 #36-66, Medellín; http://museocasadelamemoria.gov.co)

68. Stroll Through the Cartagena Botanical Garden

Cartagena is a city packed full of charm, but if you have a moment where you are overwhelmed by city life, it can be a very good idea to spend a morning strolling through the greenery of the Cartagena Botanical Garden. This is one of the best and most respected botanical gardens in all of the Caribbean region. Once you enter, you will find an area of about 20 acres with 2 kilometres of paths, 12,600 plants, trees, and orchids, and even a natural spring.

(Sector Matute km 9 Autopista I-90 (Turbaco), Naranjas; www.jbgp.org.co/en)

69. Indulge a Beer Lover at the Bogota Beer Company

If you are a beer lover through and through, there are plenty of local beers that you will want to try while you are in Colombia, but for something that little bit more special, the Bogota Beer Company is a place you have to visit. This local brewery has various locations dotted around the Colombian capital, and in each place you'll find about five really great beers on tap and more in bottles. Some locations emulate the traditional British pub look and feel. *(http://bogotabeercompany.com)*

70. Explore the Sand Dunes of Taroa

Right at the northern tip of Colombia, and indeed the northern tip of South America, you will find Punta Gallina, with extraordinary sand dunes, deserts, and indigenous culture as well. This is a place to simply enjoy walking through the desert, looking at the incredible sand dunes, and taking in a Colombian landscape that many visitors don't take the opportunity to see.

71. Catch a Show at the World's Largest International Theatre Festival

When you think of cultural capitals of the world, it is unlikely that Bogota would be the first place that springs to mind, but believe it or not, this is the city that hosts the world's largest international theatre festival. It only takes place every couple of years, so you'll have to plan to see it, but once you're in the capital there are literally thousands of different kinds of performances that you can watch. One that culture vultures shouldn't miss.

(www.festivaldeteatro.com.co)

72. Use Leticia as Your Gateway to the Colombian Amazon

When you think of the Amazon, you might well think of Brazil, but there is also plenty of the Amazon rainforest to be found in Colombia, and your gateway to this truly extraordinary part of the world is a small town of Leticia, which is home to plenty of hostels and guesthouses where you can book transportation and tours. Once you are in the Amazon, there are so many things to enjoy, so whether you'd like some tranquil birdwatching or an exciting night-time safari, there is plenty to explore.

73. Have a Fun Day at Aeroparque Juan Pablo II

If you happen to be travelling around Colombia with little ones and they aren't too keen on museum hopping, the Aeroparque Juan Pablo II is a waterpark where they are certain to have a really incredible time. There are 6 different pools inside the complex, and a tonne of waterslides, so there is really no chance of getting bored. *(Cra. 70 #16 - 04, Medellín; www.aeroparquejuanpablo.gov.co/web)*

74. Sample the Deliciousness at Paloquemao Market

Capital cities are always wonderful places to try lots of different foods. If you are in Bogota, you love to eat, and you are on a budget, Paloquemao Market is the place to be, because you can sample lots of local cuisine in one place, and you won't have to pay restaurant prices. This market is gigantic, but getting lost is half the fun. As you walk around, you can sample things like fish broth, arepas, Colombian cheese bread, and you can stock up on exotic fruits to take back to your hotel.

75. Learn Jungle Skills at Hipilandia

There are plenty of cool hostels dotted around Colombia, but Hipilandia is definitely one of coolest, because it's not just a place to sleep, but to immerse yourself in the jungle way of life and pick up some hella cool jungle skills while you're there. Whether you fancy weaving your own

backpack or you want to learn how to wield a machete, the choice is yours. Or simply relax by their natural pool.
(Cra. 9 #7-70, Leticia, Amazonas; www.hipilandia.com)

76. Purchase Some Colombian Art at Galeria Artesenal

Colombia is a country with an incredible arts and crafts culture, and what better way to always remember Colombia than to invest in some gorgeous art pieces or handmade crafts from the country? One place where you can buy really high quality items like this is the Galeria Artesenal in Bogota, which is shopping gallery with more than 80 shops, each of which is dedicated to Colombian arts and crafts. Pick up gorgeous textiles, prints, photographs, jewellery, ceramics, and more.
(Calle 16 # 5-60/70, Bogotá)

77. Visit a Replica Antioquia Village, Pueblito Paisa

Located on top of Nutibara Hill in Medellin, Pueblito Paisa is a mock Antioquia Village, created to represent how such a village would have been at the turn of the 20th century. As you walk around this village, you'll be able to see things like the town plaza, the Mayor's office, a barber shop, and a church – and all giving the feeling that you have stepped back in time. This is a great way to give kids a history lesson without having to drag them around stuffy museums.

78. Walk the Historic City Walls of Cartagena

Cartagena is a city that a lot of people visit because its coastal and you can laze on the beach or easily make your way to tropical islands from there, but it's also a place with a lot of history, and culture lovers are sure to fall in love with beautiful Cartagena as well. When the Spanish came to the "New World' they started to fortify Cartagena with walls that took two hundred years to build. You can walk along these walls and enjoy a marvellous sense of local history.

79. Hike up Mount Monserrate

When you are in Colombia's capital city, it is impossible not to notice Mount Monserrate, the mountain that dominates the skyline in virtually all parts of the city. If you are an active person, climbing this mountain is definitely an option. There are stairs the whole way to the peak, but as you'll be climbing around 600 metres, it isn't easy. If you simply want to enjoy the view from the top, there is a gondola that will transport you there.

80. Visit South America's Largest Freshwater Aquarium at Parque Explora

Parque Explora is a fantastic place to know about in Medellin if you are travelling with little ones. This interactive museum has lots of cool science stuff for kids to explore, but the jewel in its crown is a freshwater aquarium, which happens to be the largest one in all of South America. There's more than 4000 organisms to be found swimming in the aquarium, many of which are native to the waters of Colombia. You'll see piranhas, electric eels, kaleidoscopic fish, and more besides.
(Cra. 53 #7375, Medellín; www.parqueexplora.org)

81. Go White Water Rafting on the Rio Suarez

Colombia is a land of adventure. There is jungle to explore, beaches where you can do lots of water based activities, and if you really want a thrill, you can also try your hand at white water rafting on the Rio Suarez. The river experiences Class 3, 4, and 5 rapids, and if that's all French to you, it basically means that you will experience some seriously rough water – but fear not because there are lots of expert tour companies that will look after you very well and make sure you have one hell of an experience.

82. Indulge a Meat Lover With a Plate of Fritanga

Are you the type of person who is a true carnivore at heart? Then we think you'll have no problems getting along with the cuisine in Colombia, and there is a dish called fritanga that we think you will enjoy very much indeed. What we love about this dish is that it's served in a platter style with a little bit of lots of local grub. On the platter, you can expect lots of fried animal parts such as pig intestine, chorizo, black pudding, pork rinds, and lots more besides.

83. Have a Local Experience With Couchsurfing

Colombians are some of the nicest people we have ever had the pleasure of meeting, and, of course, you'll interact

with plenty of Colombians while you're on your travels, but how much cooler would it be to stay in a real Colombian home with natives of the country? This is totally possible, and free! If you're not familiar with Couchsurfing, it's a website that allows people with a spare bed or couch to connect with travellers. No money changes hands, but the benefits are not just monetary – it's also the best way to enjoy a cultural exchange.
(www.couchsuring.com)

84. Buy Beautiful Colombian Designed Things at Makeno Tienda

Colombia is a place with a lot of handicrafts and wonderfully designed items. Many of these items are very traditional, but if you fancy taking a look at something that's on the cutting edge of Colombian design, there is a shop in Medellin called Makeno Tienda that you really do have to visit. This store showcases around 90 local designers with some really cool stuff that you just won't find in other stores around Colombia. Go on – treat yourself.
(Carrera 37 # 10-35, Medellín)

85. Catch a Movie at Cine Tonala

There is so much to see and do in Colombia, but travelling can be exhausting, and there might just be times when you would like to spend a couple of hours kicking back with a great movie. When that moment strikes, Cine Tonala is undoubtedly the place to be. This is the only independent cinema in all of Bogota, so it's a place where you'll find the city's hipsters, both in the theatre and at the bar.

(Cra. 6 #35-37, Bogotá; http://cinetonala.co)

86. Go Tubing on the Palomino River

If you are someone who loves being in the great outdoors but you don't fancy anything too strenuous like climbing up a huge mountain, an incredible alternative would be to have a relaxing ride in a rubber tube, while you float along the Palomino River. The town of Palomino is located on the Caribbean coast of the country, and is the best place for this. Simply take a stroll along the riverbank and you will see multiple places that can rent you a rubber ring.

87. Play a Round of Golf in Colombia's Mountains

While Colombia certainly cannot be thought of as one of the golfing capitals of the world, it still could pay to pack your clubs as there are a few good golf courses dotted around the country. Our favourite of the bunch would have to be Club de Golf la Cima, which we like because of its very remote location up in the chilly mountains of Colombia. The course is challenging but enjoyable, and the scenery throughout is second to none.
(Club La Cima, Santa Ana, La Calera, Cundinamarca; www.clubdegolflacima.com)

88. Learn About the Colombian Currency in Bogota

You might think that learning about a country's currency is not something particularly exciting, and that all you need to know is the conversion to your home currency. Okay, so we'll concede that it's not the number one most fascinating subject in the world, but we do think that the Casa de Moneda de Colombia is a pretty cool place to visit on a grey afternoon. The most fascinating objects are the pre-Columbian exchanges, which are mostly pots, and these then lead to misshapen coins, and the coins that are known and used today.
(Cl. 11 #4-93, Bogotá, Cundinamarca)

89. Eat Hormigas Culonas if You Dare

While in Colombia, there is lots and lots of really incredible food to eat, but some of it requires a certain element of bravery to try. Hormiga Culonas is one of these foods, and the translation effectively means big-bottomed ants. These rather large leaf cutter ants are a delicacy of the country's Santander region. They are harvested in the spring time, and can be found sold on the streets or in corner shops, fried or roasted with salt. Locals swear by their aphrodisiac properties.

90. Relax Your Muscles in the Hot Springs of Santa Rosa de Cabal

Traveling around Colombia is exhilarating, but it can also be exhausting, and when you need a day of complete indulgence ad relaxation (without a whopping price tag), our favourite thing to do is unwind in the thermal springs of Santa Rosa de Cabal. There are quite a few hot springs there, and each of them has a different temperature. Entrance costs around $12, which is lower than any spa day, plus you have the joy of being surrounded by the beauty of the natural landscapes.

(www.termales.com.co)

91. Enjoy the Incredible Carnaval Celebrations of Barranquilla

Carnaval is something that is celebrated right throughout Latin America. Of course, Rio in Brazil is the place most famous for its colourful Carnaval celebrations, but did you know that the small city of Barranquilla in Colombia is said to have the second largest celebrations in all of the Latin American world? There is so much going on during this time of the year that it's impossible to list it all, but you can expect a big emphasis on Colombian folkloric tradition, with lots of cumbia dancing and music.

92. Escape City Life in Medellin's Barefoot Park

When you are looking for utter peace and tranquillity, just head to Barefoot Park in Medellin, a park which was designed with Japanese zen principles. Enter the park and you will find a sand garden, a Zen garden, a forest of bamboos, and an area of water fountains. This park was designed to be both peaceful and playful at once, so kick off your shoes and enjoy the park barefoot as intended. *(Cra. 58 #42-125, Medellín)*

93. Camp Out in the Tatacoa Desert

If you want to totally get away from the stresses of everyday life and find the idea of camping under the stars appealing, you should make yourself acquainted with the Tatacoa Desert, which is the second largest arid area in Colombia. You won't find any sand dunes here but rocky canyons that form interesting red and grey labyrinths. Something really cool is that there is a man made pool in the middle of the desert where travellers congregate to cool off in the hot sun.

94. Enjoy the Colours of Medellin's Flower Festival

During the month of August, Medellin comes to life with colour, and this is because of the annual Flower Festival that is hosted during that time of the year. Even if you aren't especially green fingered, this is a very charming time to be in the city. There is a big fireworks show to open and close the festival, equestrian events, a classic and antique cars parade, popular concerts, activities for the little ones, and lots more colourful fun besides.

95. Tuck Into a Delicious Snack of Patacones

When it's that middle of the afternoon time and you need to eat something to tide you over until having a proper meal for dinner, patacones is the snack to reach for in Colombia. This is a very simple snack of twice fried plantains, but the simplicity doesn't mean that they aren't totally delicious. These are typically served with guacamole, a chunky tomato and onion salsa, or a hot sauce for dipping.

96. Indulge a Culture Vulture at Cartagena's Hay Festival

The Hay Festival is an annual literary festival that you might have head of if you're from the UK, as this is where it started back in 1988. Since then, the festival has grown and grown, and they have international additions of the festival in various locations around the world, including the Colombian coastal city of Cartagena. The festival attracts writers and speakers from around the world, attracts around 50,000 guests each year, and is typically hosted in January.

(www.hayfestival.com/cartagena)

97. Take in the Colonial Architecture of Popayan

For somewhere a little off the beaten track in Colombia, we would highly recommend stopping into Popayan, which is located in the southwest of the country between Bogota and Quito in Ecuador. While there isn't a hell of a lot "to do" here, we think that the small city's laid back charm is a huge part of its appeal, and we love to stroll around and take in all the beauty of the gorgeous colonial architecture. Many of the buildings have a whitewashed style, and the city has been nicknamed The White City because of this.

98. Learn How to Surf on Costeno Beach

When you think of surfing destinations around the world, your mind would probably wander to places like Hawaii or Bali, but you can also find some pretty epic surf in Colombia. Our choice for a surfing destination would have to Costeno Beach, because of the great waves and because there is a Surf Camp there. Don't worry if you have absolutely no surfing experience – you can be shown the ropes right from scratch.

(http://costenobeach.com)

99. Check Out the Sculptures on Nutibara Hill

Nutibara Hill is a gorgeous untouched place in the city where you can escape city life. It is considered to be one of the seven "guardian hills" of the city, and is best known for a sculpture park that sits on top of the hill. The sculptures have been coordinated by the Museum of Modern Art in Medellin, so everything is of a very high quality, and checking this sculpture park out is a great way to have a cultural experience in the outdoors.

100. Stay Warm With a Big Hulk of Pandebono

When you think of Latin American countries, you probably always think of blue skies and hot sunshine, but Colombia has a range of temperatures, and it will be particularly chilly in the mountains. When we want some comfort food to warm us up, we always want pandebono, which is a local Colombian bread – but so much better than just another loaf. This bread is enriched with egg and salty cheese, and instead of regular flour it's made with cassava flour and cornmeal.

101. Watch a Salsa Circus Performance at Delirio

While you are in the southern city of Cali, the best choice for an unforgettable night out is at Delirio, which is self-described as a "salsa circus". It's hard to explain everything that Delirio is because it's truly a show unlike any other, but you can think of it as part salsa performance, part freakshow, and part circus extravaganza. Although the space has room for around 1500 people, it always sells out, so be sure to book your tickets in advance.

(Carrera 26 # 12 328, Centro De Eventos Valle Del Pacífico, Yumbo, Cali; www.delirio.com.co)

Before You Go

Hey you! Thanks so much for reading **101 Amazing Things to Do in Colombia**. We really hope that this helps to make your time in Colombia the most fun and memorable trip that it can be.

Have a great trip!
Team 101 Amazing Things

Printed in Great Britain
by Amazon